My Book About Bartimaeus

Based on Mark 10:46–52; Luke 18:35–43

By Mrs. Marvin Good

Illustrated by Lester M. Miller

Rod and Staff Publishers, Inc.
P.O. Box 3, Hwy. 172
Crockett, Kentucky 41413
Telephone: (606) 522-4348

SAY-IT-AGAIN SERIES

Bread and Fish
Daniel in the Lions' Den
David and Goliath
The Good Samaritan
How God Made the World
My Book About Bartimaeus
A Shepherd Boy

These books were written to provide simple, repetitious stories to be read by beginning readers who can profit by the extra repetition, or to be read to younger children whose minds can more readily grasp the content of oft-repeated material.

Copyright, 1978
By
Rod and Staff Publishers, Inc.
Crockett, Kentucky 41413

Printed in U.S.A.
ISBN 978-07399-0001-7
Catalog no. 2391

13 14 15 16 17 — 21 20 19 18 17 16 15 14 13 12

This is Bartimaeus.
He was a blind man.
He could not see.
He was blind.

See his eyes.
See Bartimaeus's eyes.
He was blind.

Bartimaeus's eyes were shut.
He could not see.
He was blind.

He could not see the birds.
He could not see the sunshine.
He could not see the flowers.
He could not see anything.

Bartimaeus was by the road.

He was waiting.

He was waiting for someone to come.

He was waiting for someone to come and give him something.

Bartimaeus was waiting for someone.

He was waiting for someone to give him something to eat.

He was blind.

He had to beg.

He had to beg for something to eat.

Bartimaeus listened.

He heard something.

He listened again.

He heard people talking.

Bartimaeus heard many people talking.

Bartimaeus heard about Jesus.

He heard what Jesus could do.

Jesus was with the people.

Bartimaeus heard Jesus.

Jesus was talking.

Jesus was talking to the people.

Bartimaeus called.

He called loudly.

He called loudly so that Jesus would hear.

Bartimaeus wanted Jesus to hear him.

Bartimaeus called, "Jesus, Son of David.

Jesus, Son of David, have mercy on me.

Jesus, have mercy on me."

The people said, "Sh-h-h.
Be still," they said.
"Sh-h-h, be still.
Do not talk so loudly.
Sh-h-h."

But Bartimaeus called again. He called loudly.

He wanted Jesus to hear.

Bartimaeus wanted Jesus to come.

Bartimaeus called again.

He called louder and louder. "Jesus, Son of David.

Jesus, Son of David, have mercy on me."

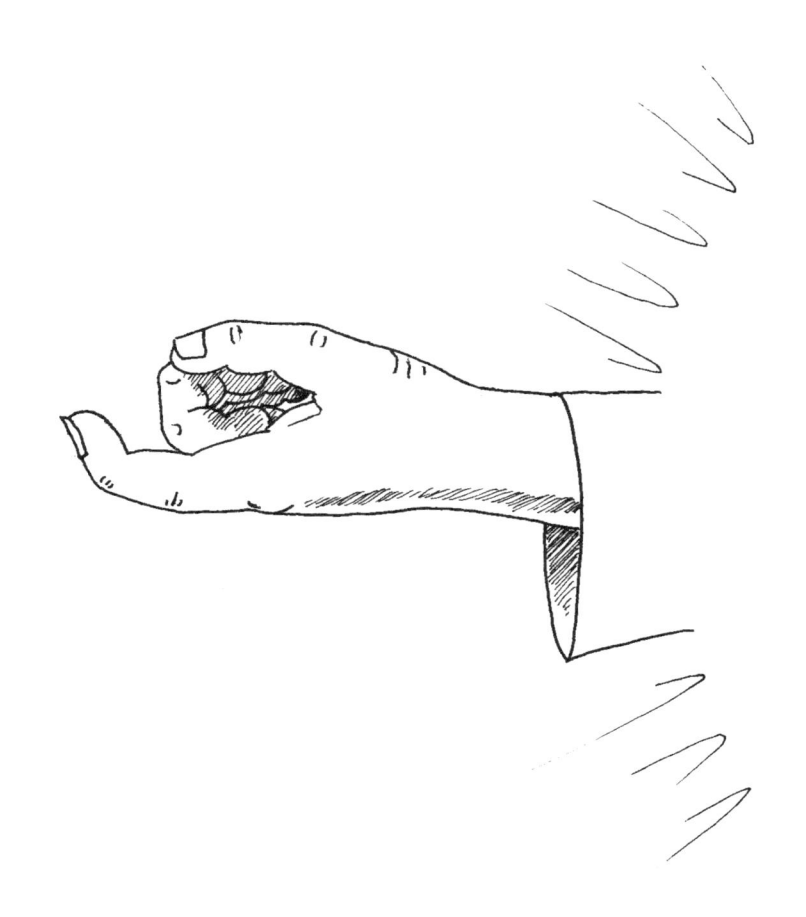

Jesus heard Bartimaeus.

Jesus stopped.

He told some men, "I want to talk to Bartimaeus. You bring him to Me."

Bartimaeus was happy.

He was happy that Jesus wanted him.

He was happy to go to Jesus.

"What shall I do?" asked Jesus.

"What do you want Me to do?

What shall I do to help you?" asked Jesus.

"Jesus, Jesus.
I cannot see.
My eyes are shut.
I am blind.

"I cannot see the birds.
I cannot see the sunshine.
I cannot see the flowers.
I cannot see anything.

"Jesus, Jesus.
Jesus, Son of David.
Open my eyes!
Open my eyes so that I can see."

Jesus said, "Your eyes are open."

Bartimaeus's eyes were opened.

Jesus opened Bartimaeus's eyes.

Now his eyes were open.
Now he can see.
He is not blind now.
Now he can see the birds.
Now he can see the sunshine.
Now he can see the flowers.
Now he can see everything.

"Thank You.

Thank You, Jesus.

Thank You, Jesus, for opening my eyes," said Bartimaeus.

"Be thankful unto him, and bless his name" (Psalm 100:4).